The Library of Tattoos and Body Piercings

Tattoos, Body Piercings, and Health

Other titles in the Library of Tattoos and Body Piercings series:

The Library
of Tattoos
and Body
Piercings

Tattoos, Body Piercings, and Health

By Leanne Currie-McGhee

ReferencePoint Press®

San Diego, CA

For more information, contact:
ReferencePoint Press, Inc.
PO Box 27779
San Diego, CA 92198
www.ReferencePointPress.com

LIBRARY OF CONGRESS CATALOGING-IN-PUBLICATION DATA

Currie-McGhee, Leanne.
  Tattoos, body piercings, and health / by Leanne Currie-McGhee.
    pages cm. -- (Library of tattoos and body piercings series)
  Includes bibliographical references and index.
  ISBN 13: 978-1-60152-564-2 (hardback)
  ISBN 10: 1-60152-564-8 (hardback)
  1. Tattooing--Health aspects--Juvenile literature. 2. Body piercing--Health aspects--Juvenile literature. I. Title.
  GN419.25.C87 2014
  391.6'5--dc23
                                                           2013009283

Contents

Introduction

Pain and Relief

To celebrate her thirty-fourth birthday, Amanda Taylor decided to get her tongue pierced. Less than forty-eight hours later, she was dead. Several people believe the cause of her death was the piercing. Taylor, of South Wales, United Kingdom, had longed to pierce her tongue for years. According to her mother, the decision to finally get pierced was a happy one for Taylor. Although her mother did not want Taylor to get pierced, she accepted the decision and told her, "You're going to be 34. I'll give you my blessing, but I'm still not 100 per cent happy."[1] Her mother now regrets giving her blessing.

Taylor went to Silverhand Jewellery in Cardiff, Wales, where a practitioner inserted a stainless steel bar less than an inch long through Taylor's tongue. At first she felt fine, but the next morning her tongue became extremely swollen, so she decided to visit a medical center. The general practitioner prescribed her antibiotics for tonsillitis. She took the medication but continued to feel poorly. At home, she collapsed and then died.

An autopsy determined that Taylor died of acute tonsillitis and septicemia, also known as blood poisoning. This is an illness that occurs when bacteria enters the bloodstream. Authorities investigated the piercing studio to see if they could link the infections to the studio itself. Of the samples they took from the studio's equipment, the police found that one sample contained bacteria resulting from poor sterilization. However, tests failed to directly link the bacteria at the piercing parlor to the bacteria that caused Taylor's sudden sickness. Even without a definitive connection, many are convinced the piercing caused her death.

Deputy coroner Liz James believes there is a clear link between the tongue piercing and Taylor's infection. According to James, "A point of entry for the infection was the piercing. Once the organism gets into the blood stream it can cause systemic streptococcus. Streptococcus is an extremely potent bacteria which, if it finds itself into the bloodstream, can very quickly lead to fatal consequences."[2]

Body Art Can Be Dangerous

Although Taylor's case is rare, it is not unheard of in today's society, where piercings and tattoos are gaining popularity. Death and serious problems can result from both. Another case similar to Taylor's occurred in 2002. A teenager, Daniel Hindle of the United Kingdom, died soon after getting a lip piercing at a studio. Days after the piercing he was hospitalized for septicemia, and he died two months later from the sickness. Hindle's girlfriend got her eyebrow pierced on the same day with him and also suffered infection from her piercing. Hindle's mother is now an advocate for more piercing regulations, and she campaigns for this cause throughout the United Kingdom.

Another teenager, Zeke Wheeler of Kansas, was hospitalized after trying to get a lip piercing. In 2008 he attempted to pierce his own lip with a first-aid kit needle, which he did not sterilize. He developed a methicillin-resistant Staphylococcus aureus (MRSA) infection, a staph infection that is difficult to counteract even with antibiotics. Wheeler almost died and needed several surgeries on his knees and hips to remove the infection, in addition to six blood transfusions.

Tattoos can also result in severe health problems. In 2012 eighteen-year-old Stephen Lister of Newberg, Oregon, tattooed two students at his high school. Lister was not a licensed tattoo artist, so he did not have training in inking tattoos or following health procedures. Both students that he tattooed ended up in the hospital battling MRSA infections.

Body artists and health professionals state that such severe health consequences from tattoos and piercings are rare. However, developing a minor problem from a piercing or tattoo is not unusual. Many tattoos and piercings result in problems such as infections and allergic reactions. Both health and body art professionals recommend that people be aware of these issues beforehand, because precautions can—and should—be taken.

Did You Know?

According to a 2010 Pew Research Center study of trends and habits, about half of the respondents with tattoos have two to five tattoos.

Body Art Benefits

On the other end of the spectrum, tattoos and piercings have been known to help people deal with certain medical issues. For example, tattoos and piercings can be used to cover up scars or transform a flawed body part into something more aesthetically pleasing to the person. This can then improve how people feel about themselves and their outlook on life.

A young woman who already has tattoos and piercings adds a tongue piercing to her body art. Many people who get piercings and tattoos have no problems other than temporary discomfort but some people experience serious health issues.

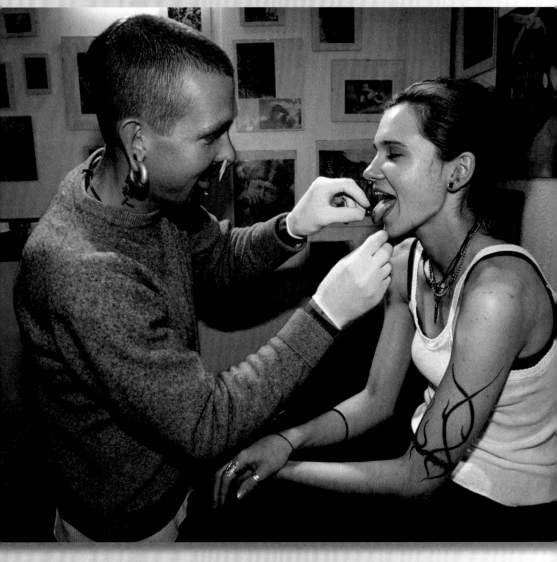

Christine Gallowan of Ohio uses her artistic talent and tattooing experience to correct the results of medical problems. Gallowan is a certified micropigmentologist, a person who tattoos cosmetic alterations to delicate areas such as the eyelids and lips. In patients who have vitiligo, a disease that results in loss of pigment coloration on the skin, Gallowan applies pigment with a tattoo machine to restore color to patches of skin that lack color. In patients who have alopecia, which results in hair loss on various parts of the body, she uses pigments to tattoo eyebrows. She can also correct the shape of a reconstructed cleft lip by restoring color to an area of the lip that is scarred. Gallowan also works with breast cancer patients. She uses her skill with a tattoo gun to recreate areolas for women who have had breast reconstruction after mastectomies.

Sheri Sweeney feels that she has regained a part of herself because of Gallowan's work. Sweeney lost her breasts to a double mastectomy that she underwent to remove her breast cancer. After reconstruction, she chose Gallowan to recreate the areolas on her "new" breasts. "I know my surgeon could have done it, but I wasn't ready then, and I'd rather have a woman who is experienced at this doing it, and whose work looks natural," says Sweeney. "There was a trust with her. I feel like Christine made me whole again."[3]

A Myriad of Issues

With body piercing and tattooing rising in popularity, body art health-related issues are also likely to increase. Body artists and health professionals suggest that those who choose to undergo the tattoo or piercing process, for whatever reason, inform themselves of both the risks and benefits of their decisions.

Chapter One

Tattooing and Body Piercing Today

If you walk down the street and glance at passersby, chances are you will see not just one, but several people who are decorated with tattoos, body piercings, or both. Decorating one's body with permanent body art has become a popular trend in today's world. Tattoos and body piercings cross all segments of society. Teenagers and adults, men and women, and people of all races are inking and piercing their bodies. Many of those who embrace this trend will find joy in their new look, but others will experience unwanted side effects or even remorse.

How Popular Is Body Art?

Tattoos were once primarily worn by those in the military, bikers, and gang members, but today people of all walks of life decorate themselves with tattoos. According to a 2012 Harris Poll examining the popularity of permanent body art, 21 percent of adults have at least one tattoo. This represents an increase in the number of people adorning themselves with tattoos, based on poll results from 2008, which found that 14 percent of people had tattoos. "It's not all about drunk teens and bikers anymore," said Jonathan Lalut, manager of Element Tattoo in Phoenix. "We had a family come in here a week ago: mom, dad and teenagers. They all got tattooed. The tattoo industry has evolved."[4]

As with tattoos, body piercings other than on the earlobes were once uncommon. But today a pierced nose, navel, tongue, or other body part hardly stands out as unusual. At Northwestern University in Chicago a study of the prevalence of tattoos and body piercings and related health issues found that about 15 percent of Americans have a piercing in a body part other than the earlobe. The majority of these people tend to be female and either teenagers or young adults. A piercer at Iron Age Studios in St. Louis, Missouri, commented on the piercing trend, "I pierce about 100 people a month, with 60 to 70 percent of them being under 18. . . . The most common place to get one is usually the navel, or ears. More girls come in to get a piercing than boys, and usually the girls can handle the process better."[5]

Tied to the rise in the popularity of body art are health issues—both minor and serious. Tattoos and body piercings can result in problems requiring a doctor's care. The Northwestern University study found that about a fourth of people with body piercings reported complications related to their piercings, such as skin infections. As for tattoos, the study found that about 13 percent of those with a tattoo reported problems with healing, such as swelling or redness, during the first two weeks after the tattoo.

What Is a Tattoo?

To get a tattoo, a person must go through a process in which his or her skin is penetrated with needles. A tattoo is a puncture wound that goes deep into the skin and is then filled with ink. A practitioner uses a tattoo machine to penetrate the skin with a needle and inject ink into the area, etching a design that the client has requested. The ink goes beyond the epidermis, the top layer of skin, into the dermis, the second, deeper layer of skin. Because dermis cells are stable, the tattoo is permanent. If the tattoo artist does not go into the dermis, the resulting tattoo will look ragged, whereas going too deep can result in bleeding and major pain.

In the past, tattoos were all done manually, with the tattoo artist puncturing the skin with a needle and injecting the ink by hand. Today most tattoos are done with a handheld electric machine; on one end of the machine is a needle, which is attached to tubes of ink. When turned on, the needle moves in and out and drives the ink just under the skin. Getting a tattoo can take minutes to hours, depending on the size and complexity of the design.

The tattooing process is vulnerable to complications because the tattoo is a wound in the skin, where bacteria and dirt can enter the body. If this happens, the bacteria or dirt can cause an infection. Also, a virus can enter the wound and result in a serious disease. Another problem that can occur is that the dyes that enter the skin can cause allergic reactions.

People who get piercings or tattoos do not fit a specific type. Sometimes whole families seek tattoos together, while teens and young adults are more likely to get piercings than other age groups.

Even as the skin heals, scars, swelling, and other skin problems can result. The chances of these problems occurring are greatly increased if the person giving the tattoo is not a licensed tattoo artist. Unlike a licensed artist, an unlicensed practitioner may not be trained in how to reduce the chances of a person developing health issues.

Body Piercing Process

As with tattoos, body piercings can also result in a variety of health complications. To create a piercing, a practitioner uses a needle to puncture the desired body part and then inserts jewelry into the puncture. Typical body parts that are pierced include the upper ears, nostrils, navel, and tongue. But some people also request piercing of the eyebrow, lips, cheeks, nipples, and even genitalia.

The risk of infection exists with piercings just as it does with tattoos: bacteria, dirt, or a virus can enter the puncture point and cause an infection. Scarring and allergic reactions are other possible side effects of piercings. According to nurse JoAnn Nester, "You can get any blood borne disease, Hepatitis A & B and even HIV [human immunodeficiency virus] from piercings. There is always the risk of infections, even if it's done correctly."[6]

Source of Problems

One major source of health problems related to piercings and tattoos is the number of unlicensed tattoo artists and body piercers who are performing these procedures. Licensed practitioners are required to follow city health codes and also are often required to take courses that teach them how to prevent spreading infection and disease. Unlicensed tattooists and body piercers, on the other hand, are less likely to have any training in proper techniques and might very well be ignorant of city and state hygiene codes.

People choose to go to unlicensed practitioners for different reasons. One is that unlicensed tattoo artists and body piercers are often less expensive than licensed ones. Teenagers often choose to get a tattoo or body piercing from an unlicensed practitioner to avoid laws

Did You Know?

Twenty-three percent of eighteen- to twenty-nine-year-olds report having a piercing somewhere other than the earlobe, according to a 2010 Pew Research Center study.

that require them to provide written parental consent or have a parent present in the studio during the tattooing or piercing procedure. For whatever reason, many people end up getting their body art by unlicensed practitioners, and this increases health risks.

Different studies have linked health problems specifically to unlicensed body art practitioners. In 2006 the Centers for Disease Control and Prevention reported that it linked forty-four cases of potentially serious antibiotic-resistant skin infections to unlicensed tattoo artists who did not follow proper infection-control procedures. These antibiotic-resistant skin infections can lead to pneumonia, bloodstream infections, and a painful, flesh-destroying condition called necrotizing fasciitis.

Shane Warnke, a tattoo artist in Iowa, has seen a rise in unlicensed tattoo work over the past few years and the problems resulting from this trend. He states that about 60 percent of his work is fixing botched tattoos by unlicensed tattoo artists. Additionally, he worries about the health problems that unlicensed work causes. Before becoming a professional tattoo artist, Warnke got a tattoo from an unlicensed person and now realizes what a poor job the person did in terms of sterilization. He says, "They had needles they'd used on other people sitting in a sauce pan in boiling water on the stove, and I remember asking, 'What's the purpose of this?' They said, 'I'm sterilizing everything.' You know, I know now that that ain't going to do nothing."[7] To become a licensed artist, Warnke had to learn the proper sterilization procedures needed to protect clients.

Living with Disease

Among the most serious problems that can result from a tattoo or body piercing are diseases that are transmitted by viruses in the blood. Although the reported cases of any of these diseases being linked to tattoos and piercings is low, health professionals stress the possibility that these can occur. According to the Mayo Clinic, "If the equipment used to do the piercing is contaminated with infected blood, you can contract various bloodborne diseases—including hepatitis B, hepatitis C, tetanus and HIV."[8] Of these, hepatitis C, which can severely damage the liver, is most likely.

A tattoo artist in London creates an elaborate and colorful design. As shown here, most tattoos are done with a handheld electric machine, with a needle on one end and tubes of ink attached at the other end.

Actress Pamela Anderson discovered she contracted hepatitis C in 2002 and believes a tattoo was the cause. Hepatitis C is a disease that leads to swelling of the liver. This can lead to cirrhosis, or severe scarring, of the liver, which can eventually result in liver failure. There are medications available to help combat the virus and keep the liver healthy. Anderson has stated that she and her then husband, Tommy Lee of Motley Crüe, shared a tattoo needle. Since then she has suffered from the disease and will likely have to deal with it the rest of her life, because 75 to 85 percent of hepatitis C cases becomes a chronic affliction. When she was first diagnosed, Anderson feared she would die in ten to fifteen years, but since then she has been able to maintain her liver's health through the latest treatments. However, the treatments themselves are difficult to endure. In 2009 Anderson decided to get antiviral injections to help keep her liver healthy even though the injections would cause pain. "There's lots of side effects." she told CNN's Larry King before starting the treatments. "It's going to be a year of basically having the flu. Your hair falls out. It's a little kind of chemotherapy."[9]

No Experience Necessary

In the past decade there has been a rise in unlicensed tattoo artists and body piercers partly due to the ease of obtaining equipment. Tattoo machines and associated equipment once available only to licensed studios can now be purchased from online vendors by almost anyone. Also, body piercing needles and jewelry are available on the Internet. Even some brick-and-mortar stores sell tattoo or piercing equipment without asking customers for a practitioner's license. A relatively new kiosk business at the Westfield Annapolis Mall in Maryland sells piercing rings and tattoo equipment such as tattoo guns, needles, and ink to anyone age twenty-one or older. The buyer need not have any experience in tattooing or body piercing and is not required to demonstrate any knowledge of state health regulations.

Body Art Allergies

Another potential problem with getting a tattoo or piercing is developing an allergic reaction to the body art. A person's skin may develop a rash or itch due to the inks used in the tattoo. Some people may experience hives or red sores because of the type of jewelry used in a piercing.

A tattoo allergy is caused by the body's reaction to an ingredient in the tattoo ink. Tattoo inks can be made with a combination of different ingredients and chemicals. Some of the ingredients that are more prone to cause allergic reactions are iron oxide, mercury sulfide, ferric hydrate, aluminum, and manganese. Studies have found that red tattoo ink is the most likely color to produce an allergy. Typically, a tattoo allergy results in swelling, irritation, a rash, or other skin abnormality around the site of the tattoo.

In many cases ointment—and time—can take care of a tattoo allergy. However, in more serious cases an infection may result from the allergy and require antibiotics. In the worst cases tattoo removal is the only way to eliminate the allergic reaction.

Piercings can also result in allergic reactions if the person is allergic to the material in the jewelry that is used. One of the most common jewelry materials to cause reactions is nickel. According to the Mayo Clinic, "Once you develop a sensitivity to nickel, you will develop a rash (contact dermatitis) whenever you come into contact with the metal. Once an allergic reaction to nickel exposure has begun, it will most likely continue for two to four weeks."[10] Allergic reactions from piercings may include swelling, redness, itching, and hives. Additionally, eczema, an inflammation of the skin, and dermatitis, a blistering of the skin, can result from an allergic reaction.

With piercings, the allergic reaction can be alleviated relatively easily. The first step is to change the jewelry to a material that does not cause an allergic reaction. As the skin heals from the reaction, a topical ointment for the skin may also be prescribed to help the process. Eventually, the skin will return to a healthy state if these procedures are followed.

A practitioner who does not follow proper sanitation procedures risks infecting clients with blood-borne diseases such as hepatitis C, which can severely damage the liver. Pictured is a hepatitis-infected liver.

Prevention

The best protection against infection and other problems after getting a tattoo or piercing is to follow the practitioner's aftercare instructions. For tattoos, typical aftercare procedures include leaving a bandage over the tattoo for at least two hours. This prevents bacteria and dirt from entering the wound. After the bandage is taken off, tattoo professionals recommend that the person gently wash the tattoo with a mild antibacterial soap. Then they recommend that the person lightly dry the tattoo and rub an ointment over it. Professionals recommend that people with new tattoos continue to do this periodically over the next three days and after that use a lotion on the tattoo. Additionally, health professionals recommend not picking or scratching the tattoo and keeping it completely out of the sun for at least the first two weeks and keeping it out of sustained sunlight for three months.

As for body piercings, Elayne Angel, author of *The Piercing Bible*, recommends that newly pierced individuals follow strict aftercare procedures to avoid infections. Some piercings take months before they fully heal, and strict aftercare procedures should be maintained the entire time, she writes. To keep the piercings healthy, Angel recommends that during the healing process a person apply a paper towel soaked in saline solution to the piercing for five minutes a day. She also suggests that people only touch their piercings with washed hands and pat them dry after any shower or bath. Following her tips will increase the chance of the piercing healing properly.

Medical Uses for Body Art

For most people body art represents a desired look, style, or form of personal expression. For some people, however, it addresses a medical need or condition. People with medical conditions such as diabetes or epilepsy sometimes wear medical bracelets that identify their condition in case they are incapacitated by a seizure or other medical event. The bracelets tell emergency medical personnel about their condition, which allows a quicker and safer

When Teens Lack Discipline

Elayne Angel, master piercer and author of two piercing books, has no problem with teens getting pierced, provided they choose knowledgeable piercers and follow aftercare procedures. However, she has found that many teens are not diligent about aftercare—and that often leads to complications. She writes:

> One of the common risks found with younger people (even those who do get a quality piercing) is that they may lack the discipline required to care for the piercing throughout an extended duration of healing. So they might change their jewelry too soon, which represents risks of infection, irritation, and healing problems. Also, they may become tired of doing the cleanings, and stop, which also represents risk of infection.

Angel stresses that healing can take as long as six to nine months. She says that teens need to be ready to follow procedures for this amount of time if they want their piercing to stay healthy.

Elayne Angel, "Piercing Risks to Teenagers," *The Piercing Bible* (blog), October 2010. http://piercingbible.com.

response. In some instances people with these conditions have tattooed the information on their bodies to make sure it is always available to emergency responders.

Michelle Bryant believes that her tattoo saved her life. An asthmatic, in 2012 Bryant became ill in a store. When the employees saw her tattoo of a MedicAlert symbol and the word *asthma*, they immediately called for an ambulance. According to Bryant, "I had almost stopped breathing by the time the paramedics arrived. Without my tattoo, I do not think I would be alive today. I could not tell anyone what was happening, but the tattoo showed the staff what the problem was, I didn't have to say a word."[11]

The Future of Tattoos and Piercings

As tattoos and piercings have become more popular, the potential health risks and benefits of both have come to light. On one hand, when people adorn themselves with body art, they put themselves at a higher risk for a range of problems. At the same time, the popularity of these types of body art has resulted in discoveries of ways tattoos and piercings can help people both physically and emotionally. Tattoos and body piercings will continue to have effects on people's health as the trend to decorate oneself with permanent art continues.

Chapter Two

Tattoo Health Risks

Imagine a needle puncturing your skin hundreds of times a second. This is what happens when a person gets tattooed. Dragos Roua recalls getting his first tattoo in 2011. He did not know what to expect and soon found he had to endure two hours of pain before emerging with a tattoo of a scorpion on his arm. "If you're a normal person, getting a tattoo hurts. By normal person I mean one with a regular nerve and skin structure. . . . I'm a normal person and my skin nerves are performing exactly as they should do: informing me of every aggression that might happen, by triggering pain."[12]

Pain is not the only difficult part of getting a tattoo. During and after the tattoo process, the punctures in the skin are vulnerable to germs. Germs can lead to infections and other conditions, ranging from minor to deadly.

The Worst Case

When a person gets a tattoo from a reputable, licensed artist who follows proper hygiene procedures, the chance of becoming infected with a viral disease is low, according to medical agencies such as the Centers for Disease Control and Prevention (CDC). However, if a person gets a tattoo from someone who does not follow hygienic procedures, the likelihood of contracting a blood-borne disease increases. This can happen when tattooists do not use brand-new needles for each person or if they reuse needles that have not been properly sanitized. "Only sterile equipment should be used for

Did You Know?

A tattoo machine moves a solid needle up and down to puncture the skin between fifty and three thousand times per minute.

tattooing or body piercing,"[13] the CDC states. When sanitary practices are not followed, viruses from one person can be transmitted to another through the needle.

The blood-borne infections and diseases of greatest concern are tetanus, hepatitis C, hepatitis B, and HIV. The most serious of these is HIV, a viral infection that harms the immune system and may develop into the potentially fatal illness, acquired immune deficiency syndrome, or AIDS. The CDC notes that tattooing presents a potential risk of HIV transmission, although no cases of HIV transmission from tattooing have actually been documented. One reason for this might be that fact that the virus that causes AIDS does not live long outside of the body, which makes it difficult to transmit via tattoo needles. The more easily transmitted blood-borne illnesses are hepatitis B and hepatitis C. Hepatitis B is a serious disease because it can damage the liver to the point that a transplant may be required. Hepatitis C results in inflammation of the liver, which can lead to scarring and a breakdown of the liver's functioning. About 70 percent of people infected with hepatitis C will develop chronic liver disease, and up to 5 percent will die from cirrhosis or liver cancer.

Of the blood-borne diseases, studies have linked hepatitis C to tattooing more than any other. In 2013 results from a study by Dr. Fritz Francois of the New York University Langone Medical Center found that people with hepatitis C were more likely to have a tattoo than people without the disease. For this study, researchers questioned nearly two thousand people about their tattoos and hepatitis status at outpatient clinics at three New York area hospitals between 2004 and 2006.

The most-documented ways that people have contracted hepatitis C is through a blood transfusion prior to 1992 or by injected drug use. But 20 percent of hepatitis C cases have no history of either of these. Francois and his colleagues only included people with hepatitis C who claimed they did not contract the disease from either of the two common sources. Of the people they surveyed, the researchers discovered that those with tattoos were almost four times more likely to have hepatitis C than those

Did You Know?

The Red Cross prohibits a person who has received a tattoo from donating blood for twelve months unless the procedure was done in a state-regulated and licensed studio, using sterile techniques.

22

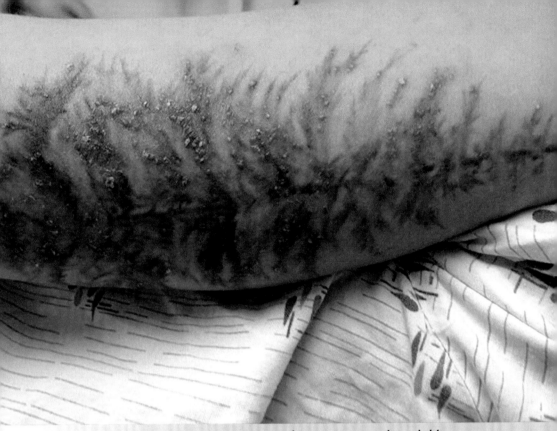

An infection resulting from a tattoo turned into a nasty rash with blisters on the client's arm. Because the tattoo process involves puncturing the skin, people getting tattoos are vulnerable to germs and infection.

without tattoos. However, the study did not take into account whether professional or amateur tattoo artists did the work. Organizations such as the CDC have stated that the risk for blood-borne diseases among unlicensed artists is much greater than with professionals. But whether the tattoos were by unlicensed individuals or not, the study indicates that hepatitis C is a risk for people getting tattoos.

Other Infections

Although blood-borne viral infections are the most serious afflictions that can result from tattoos, they are not the most common. A more common problem is bacterial infections, which can range from minor to serious. Minor infections are ones that the body can fight off on its own, without medicine or other care. Typically, a minor infection from tattooing will result in redness and itching and clears up over time with proper hygiene.

MRI Interference

One unusual complication with tattoos is that in some cases the metals in tattoo inks may sting or burn when people undergo magnetic resonance imaging (MRI) exams. An MRI uses magnetic waves to "see" internal organs without using an X-ray. Although the instances have been few and mostly anecdotal, doctors and health organizations have put out warnings regarding the possibility that an MRI might affect a tattoo. In a few documented cases, MRIs have caused swelling or burning in the tattooed areas. Also, in some cases tattoos have interfered with the quality of the image. However, doctors stress that the risks of avoiding an MRI when it has been recommended are much greater than the risks of any reaction that might occur.

More serious infections result in boils or swelling and require antibiotics. Still other infections can lead to extreme pain and cause major illnesses if untreated. These infections may require stronger antibiotics taken over a long period and, in extreme situations, having the tattoo excised by a doctor. In this situation a surgeon surgically removes the tattooed skin, then stitches the remaining skin back together. The severity of an infection is determined by what types of germs caused the infection and how a person's immune system reacts to it.

Anyone getting a tattoo is susceptible to developing an infection, even during the healing process. "Oftentimes, you think about the actual tattooing as a means for infection," said Will Humble, director of the Arizona Department of Health Services. "In reality, there are so many other opportunities for infection, including the tattooed person not properly cleaning the wound."[14] At any stage of the tattoo process, if proper procedures are not followed, the chances of contracting an infection are greatly increased.

Extreme Infection

Other infections are so extreme that hospitalization is needed. For example, Susan Fraser of Scotland was hospitalized and almost lost her foot because of a tattoo infection. While traveling to Turkey in 2012, Fraser decided to get a tattoo of vines, leaves, and hearts on her foot. She chose a studio in Marmaris, a popular Turkish resort town. A few hours after getting the tattoo, her foot swelled and became so painful that she could barely walk. Fraser returned to the tattoo studio and showed them her foot. The tattoo artist told her the swelling must have been the result of salt water reacting with the tattoo and rubbing from her sandals. However, Fraser knew the problem was more serious than that because her foot was oozing blood and extremely swollen.

Fraser returned home and was immediately taken to the hospital. She remained there for a month while doctors treated the infection. It resisted three intravenous antibiotic courses, and at that point her doctors considered amputation. However, after one more course of antibiotics, her foot finally healed. But Fraser must live with permanent damage to her skin. "It looks like scar tissue and turns really red, especially when I've been on my feet for a while,"[15] she says.

Serious Outbreak

In 2012 a serious outbreak of infections resulting from tattoos occurred in several states. In these cases the infection entered the people's bodies through the ink that was injected in their skin. An investigation conducted by the CDC found twenty-two confirmed cases, four probable cases, and twenty-seven possible cases of contamination-related tattoo infections in New York, Washington, Iowa, and Colorado. The tattoo artists in the study followed proper hygiene procedures, but infections still occurred because the tattoo ink they purchased was contaminated. The study found that bacteria had entered containers that the tattoo ink manufacturer used for distilled water, which was used to dilute certain tattoo inks.

The bacteria that caused the New York cases was *Mycobacterium chelonae*; it resulted in reddish or purple raised bumps in the areas tattooed with gray ink. This type of infection looks similar to an allergic reaction, making it difficult to diagnose. For those who were diagnosed, it took lengthy treatment to heal their infections. "They were not getting better," said Dr. Byron Kennedy of the Monroe County Department of Public

Public health officials have expressed concerns about the safety of some inks used in tattooing. They are concerned about potentially harmful ingredients used in making the inks and also about the possible long-term effects of tattoo ink on certain parts of the body.

Health when speaking of the first treatment of antibiotics given to the infected people. "You had some folks who were on treatment for 6 months or more."[16] Some of those who contracted the infection required several courses of antibiotics before they were cured.

Ink Issues

Tattoo inks may also be a source of other health problems due to their chemical makeup. Many doctors are concerned about the ingredients in tattoo ink because some ink has been linked to potentially serious health issues. A 2011 study found that toxic chemicals such as phthalates, metals, and hydrocarbons can be found in tattoo inks. These are of concern because in various tests they have resulted in health problems. For example, benzo(a)pyrene, one of the chemicals found in black tattoo inks, is a strong carcinogen, a chemical that has caused skin cancer in animal experiments. Health professionals believe there could be a link between skin cancers in humans and tattoos as well.

There is uncertainty about the dangers of tattoo ink ingredients because no official study has found a definitive link between health problems and tattoo inks. However, there is enough concern that the US Food and Drug Administration (FDA) decided to investigate tattoo inks and how they affect the body. At an FDA laboratory in Arkansas, research chemist Paul Howard and his team are investigating tattoo inks to determine what their chemical composition is and how they are broken down in the body. They are also researching the short-term and long-term safety of the pigments used in the inks and how the pigments respond to light exposure. "There have been no systematic studies of the safety of tattoo inks," says Howard, "so we are trying to ask—and answer—some fundamental questions."[17] As an example, they want to discover what happens to tattoo inks when they fade over time due to the sun and what happens when laser light removes tattoos. Howard and his team are searching for the answer to how the body absorbs the ink and where the ink ends up.

Another concern about tattoo ink is that studies have found the inks migrate into the lymph nodes. Lymph nodes are part of the lymphatic system, which filters out disease-causing organisms. What is unknown is if the tattoo ink negatively affects this system or not. Until answers are found about the effects of tattoo pigments on lymph nodes and other parts of the body, the FDA recommends that people carefully consider whether or not to get a tattoo.

Scarring

Scarring is another health-related tattoo issue. If a tattoo artist goes too deep into the skin and/or uses excessive force when tattooing, the person getting the tattoo can end up with a visible scar. Another factor is that some people take longer to heal than others and as a result are more susceptible to scars. Scarring may not occur immediately after tattooing but instead become evident in the weeks or months after the tattoo has healed. A symptom of severe scarring is patches of discolored skin that can even be seen under the tattoo. Severe scars can cause the tattoo's colors to run, caus-

Did You Know?

A 2010 study of health incidents among tattooed people in German-speaking countries printed in *Dermatology* found that approximately 5 percent of nearly six thousand individuals who received a tattoo reported some bleeding.

ing the darker shades to mix with the lighter shades. Or skin may become uneven, puffy, and raised near the tattoo.

The most noticeable types of scars that can result from tattooing include keloids, fleshy dark-colored tissue that protrudes from the skin and extends beyond the original scarred area. Another is hypertrophic scars, which are red, thick, and also raised, but not as much as keloids. Keloids and hypertrophic scars can result from piercings, tattoos, and any other type of skin injury. Keloids often require no treatment and may flatten over time. However, keloids can grow as much as 1 inch (2.5 cm) above the skin. In cases such as this, they might need to be reduced in size by freezing (cryotherapy), external pressure, corticosteroid injections, laser treatments, radiation, or surgical removal. Even when removed, it is not unusual for keloids to reappear. Hypertrophic scars are typically more responsive to treatments than keloids and can often be flattened and become lighter in color with similar nonsurgical treatments as keloids. The tendency toward these types of scars is inherited, so certain people are more likely to develop them than others. Also, these kinds of scars are more common in people with dark skin, but a person of any skin color can develop them. Doctors recommend that people who are prone to keloids or hypertrophic scars not get tattooed, because of the increased chance that they will develop such scars.

Increased Risk

Getting a tattoo can be riskier for some people than others. People with diabetes and women who are pregnant are in this group and, according to tattoo artists, should always consult their doctors before getting a tattoo.

Diabetics who decide to get tattoos need to take extra precautions because their wounds often take longer to heal, and a longer healing time makes these individuals more susceptible to infections. People with diabetes also need to ensure their blood sugar level is not high when they get a tattoo, because high blood sugar can slow healing. Also, S. William

Levy, professor of dermatology at the University of California–San Francisco Medical Center, warns that diabetics need to avoid getting tattoos on certain parts of the body. These include areas with poor circulation, such as ankles and the lower legs, and areas of the body where a diabetic takes his or her insulin shot. On several blogs, diabetics who chose to get tattoos wrote that they ensured their blood sugar was at an appropriate level before getting the tattoo. Some who had gotten tattoos before they were diagnosed with diabetes noticed that when they got a tattoo after their diagnosis, the tattoo took longer to heal than previous ones.

Many doctors say that women should not get tattoos while they are pregnant. This is because so much is still unknown about the skin dyes used in tattooing. It is possible that the chemicals in the dyes might affect the development of the fetus, especially during the first twelve weeks of pregnancy. Experts are concerned that infections contracted during the tattoo process could also affect the fetus.

Qualified and licensed tattoo artists follow strict sanitation procedures including wearing gloves while working. Such procedures help protect both clients and practitioners from the spread of germs.

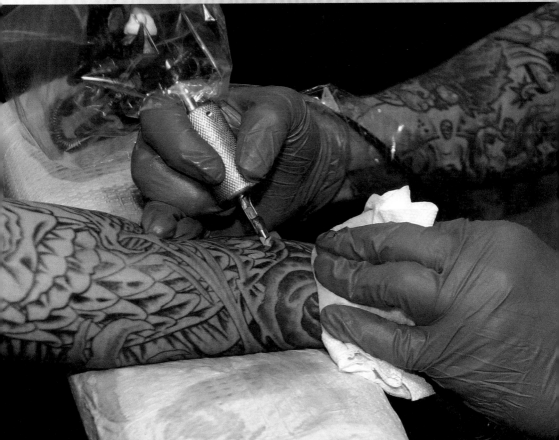

Education and Training

Many states have adopted laws intended to make tattooing safer. These laws vary from state to state, but many specifically require training in sterilization practices, a course on blood pathogens and how to prevent them, and professional training such as an apprenticeship under a licensed tattoo artist. Once all training is completed, in most cases practitioners can obtain a license. Certain states have even more stringent requirements. For example, California requires that people seeking a license to tattoo must prove they are vaccinated against and free of hepatitis B.

Of all the training required, a blood-borne pathogens class is the most common because of the need to protect people from serious blood-borne diseases. The American Red Cross is one of the organizations that conduct a course for tattoo artists on blood-borne pathogens. The course teaches how such pathogens spread, how to avoid being exposed and exposing others to them, and what to do if someone is exposed to infectious material. The course can be taken online or in person and is approximately two hours long. When tattoo artists complete the training from the American Red Cross, they receive certification for one year.

Tattoo studios in most localities are also required to comply with local health codes. These health codes typically include adherence to ster-

Not a Good Mix

Some bleeding is common during the tattooing process because the needle is puncturing the skin. In most cases this is not cause for concern. But it can be a problem in someone who is taking a blood thinner to help prevent formation of blood clots or for other reasons. A person who is taking a blood thinner is more likely to bleed heavily if cut. In the case of tattoos, the danger is excessive bleeding when the needle punctures the skin. This can mar the look of the person's tattoo and, more seriously, harm a person's health.

ilization of equipment and proper disposal of waste. The eHow website explains tattoo studio regulations: "In most states, laws outline the type of tools that can be used to tattoo; how those tools should be cleaned or disposed of; and how the studio itself should be cleaned and maintained. Studios may be required to have an autoclave sterilizer on hand for reusable materials, and hazardous waste collection receptacles for those that are disposable."[18]

Ultimately, people who get tattoos put themselves at risk for health issues, although there are ways to reduce these risks. Before getting a tattoo, people can educate themselves on what the risks are, what their personal risks may be, and what the long-term effects of tattoos are.

Chapter Three

Body Piercing Health Risks

Because body piercing, by definition, means puncturing the skin, infection is always a possibility. And because some piercings—for example, navel piercings—take months to heal, the chance of infection is high. Even so, it is possible to minimize the risks.

Complications

Germs, specifically certain types of bacteria and viruses, are what cause most of the problems associated with body piercings. Germs on the needle used to pierce a person may transfer from the needle into the person's body through the piercing wound. Using nonsterile equipment greatly increases the likelihood of transmitting germs to the person receiving the piercing. Germs can also enter the opening during healing, thus leading to infection.

Complications from piercing also have other causes. An allergic reaction to the material used in the jewelry can produce redness or itching. Also, if a piece of jewelry gets caught on something, it can tear the skin. Other possible problems include chipped teeth from tongue piercings and skin discoloration from navel piercings.

All of these complications are fairly common, as studies have shown. In 2008 the British Health Protection Agency and the London School of Hygiene and Tropical Medicine completed a study on body piercing. This study included more than 10,000 people. Of those surveyed, 28 percent of piercings in body parts other than the earlobe led to complications, with one in one hundred piercings resulting in a hospital admission.

Serious Medical Conditions

The worst-case scenario for someone getting pierced is that he or she develops a serious health problem as a result of a virus. As with tattoos, blood-borne diseases are a possibility. Hepatitis B, hepatitis C, and HIV viruses can be transmitted from the needle into the person's body via the piercing wound. As with tattoos, these incidences are low but possible, and the risk is higher when unsterilized equipment is used.

Another serious medical condition that can result from a piercing is endocarditis, an inflammation of the inside lining of the heart chambers caused by germs entering the bloodstream and traveling to the heart. Bacterial infection is the most common cause of endocarditis and can result from a piercing. The most serious effects of endocarditis are heart failure and stroke. In 2011 an article in the *Journal of Medical Case Reports* discussed how a twenty-nine-year-old Korean woman developed endocarditis after an earlobe piercing. She recovered after cardiac surgery and eight weeks of antibiotics.

Nerve damage caused by accidentally puncturing a nerve is another problem that can result from piercing. The result of nerve damage may be a loss of feeling or control of that particular area of the body. For example, an eyebrow piercing can result in partial paralysis of the face if a major nerve is struck.

Watch the Mouth

The lips, cheeks, and tongue are becoming popular spots for body piercing, but all three can lead to various health problems. In fact, the American Dental Association has come out strongly against all types of oral piercings, due to the many complications that can result. These range from minor to severe issues.

One of the most dangerous problems of a tongue piercing is that it can result in Ludwig's angina, an infection of the mouth that is potentially fatal. Ludwig's angina is caused by a bacterium that enters the bloodstream through the mouth. In the case of a tongue piercing, the

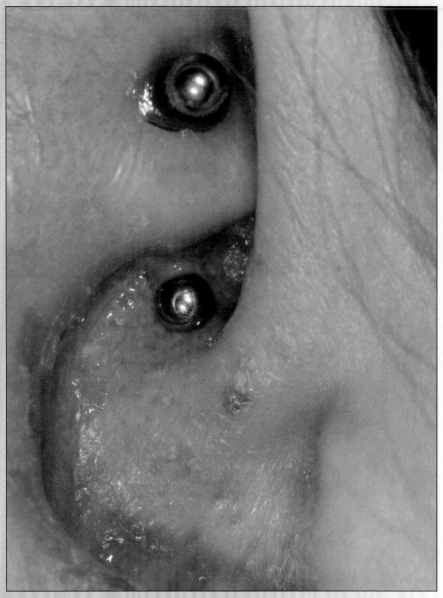

Ear piercings show signs of infection in this twenty-two-year-old woman. Complications from piercings can result from allergic reactions to the jewelry or, in more serious cases, from contaminated equipment.

bacterium enters through the piercing wound. This affliction generally results in swelling of the mouth to the point that a person cannot breathe unless he or she receives immediate medical attention.

Another serious issue related to tongue piercings is excessive bleeding. This is due to the fact the tongue is filled with many blood vessels.

During a tongue piercing, if the practitioner punctures a blood vessel, prolonged bleeding can occur. Fifteen-year-old Reece-Marie Hall of Great Britain discovered this after she had her tongue pierced at a studio and the silver bar that was placed in her tongue ruptured a vein. "At first my tongue didn't bleed, but after I left the shop the tongue started pouring with blood. I kept choking,"[19] Hall said. She was rushed to the hospital, and doctors had to surgically remove the jewelry after putting her under general anesthesia.

The American Dental Association also links piercing to speech impediments, tongue swelling that can impede breathing, gum recession where the gums recede to the point that they expose the roots of the teeth, and accidental swallowing of jewelry, which can result in choking. Chipped and cracked teeth are another common occurrence in people who have tongue piercings. A story in the *Journal of Periodontology* reported that 47 percent of people wearing barbell tongue jewelry for four or more years had at least one chipped tooth.

Lastly, lip piercings can also result in gum problems. If a piece of metal is inserted through the lip, it will come in contact with the gums. Many lip piercings rub the gums and result in the gums receding. Receding gums can lead to tooth decay and also expose the tooth's nerve endings. This can lead to a person becoming extremely sensitive to cold and hot foods or liquids in their mouth, which can produce pain. Receding gums can be corrected, but only if the piercing is completely removed.

Dealing with a Major Infection

The risk of infection from a piercing is higher than for tattoos because the healing process for piercings takes longer. For example, a tongue piercing, among the fastest to heal, takes one to two months to heal, and navel and nipple piercings, among the slowest to heal, take approximately nine months to heal. According to a 2012 research paper published by Dr. Anne Laumann, chief of dermatology at Northwestern University's Feinberg School of Medicine in Chicago, approximately 20

Did You Know?

A 2008 British Health Protection Agency and London School of Hygiene and Tropical Medicine study found that self-piercings and those not carried out by a specialist were more likely to require medical attention.

percent of piercings result in bacterial infections. However, according to the paper, most of these infections are localized and can be easily treated.

At age sixteen, Shanay (last name not given) discovered how much damage a piercing infection can do. After getting permission from her mother, she decided to get her navel pierced. Navel piercings take the longest time to heal and are the most prone to infection because clothing rubs against the piercing, which can irritate the wound. In spite of this, naval piercings are quite popular.

At first, Shanay was pleased with her piercing, but her pleasure soon turned to pain. A week later, her piercing got stuck on a piece of her clothing, and the piercing tore and bled. From that point on, more prob-

Don't Touch the Cheek

Elayne Angel, master piercer, has many piercings on her body. However, even she will not pierce certain areas of the body, due to the difficulties of healing. One area she does not pierce is the cheeks, stemming from her own bad experience with cheek piercing. She relates, "On November 13, 1998 I pierced my own cheeks, directly in the fairly pronounced dimples I already had. I had thought about this piercing for many years, fantasizing about wearing diamonds in my dimples." Angel was happy with her piercings until one and a half years later, when her cheek started to leak fluid. It continued to the point that she had to remove the piercings at a doctor's recommendation. "My right cheek continued to leak off and on over the ensuing months, even after I took the jewelry out. I had to try something drastic. I used a medical tool called a cautery scalpel to burn the hole shut by generating scar tissue. . . . That worked for a few weeks, but then the leaking started yet again. It finally sealed completely after using the cautery scalpel for the third time, creating a deeper and more severe burn." As a result of this experience, she will not pierce anyone's cheeks beyond the molar area.

Elayne Angel, "Cheek Piercing Dangers," *The Piercing Bible*, 2009. http://piercingbible.com.

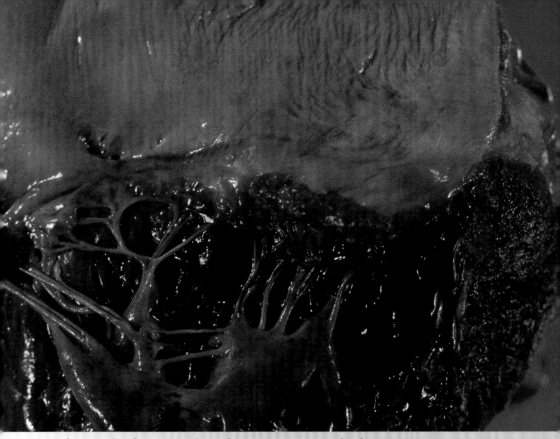

A bacterial infection resulting from a piercing can lead to a serious condition known as endocarditis. This close-up view shows the inflamed inner lining of the heart, which is characteristic of this condition.

lems occurred. First, blood and greenish pus started to ooze from the opening, which was also sore to the touch. She began to experience stomachaches, and the skin around her navel blackened. At this point her mother took her to the doctor, and the end result was the removal of her piercing. "The doctor told me that the only way to fix it was to surgically remove it and close the hole," Shanay wrote. "After my surgery, they told me never to get one again. . . . My dream birthday gift turned into my nightmare."[20]

Worst-Case Infection

Stephanie Edington of Indiana had an even worse experience with her piercing. Edington decided to have both of her nipples pierced to celebrate her eighteenth birthday. A few weeks after getting pierced, her left breast became tender, red, and extremely painful. Edington went to the

St. Clare Medical Center emergency room in Indianapolis; she was immediately admitted for treatment.

She was diagnosed with an infection, which continued to worsen. Two days after being admitted, Edington was diagnosed with necrotizing fasciitis, a bacteria growth that destroys tissue. Because of the seriousness of her condition, doctors transferred her to Indiana University Medical Center for surgery. Doctors there removed one breast, lymph nodes, and skin up to her collarbone to rid her body of the infection. "You have no idea what it's like to almost lose your daughter and then to make the decision to have one of her breasts removed," Edington's mother, Pamela Osban, said. "Some people say, 'It's just a breast.' They aren't an 18-year-old girl. It's devastating for her and for the family."[21]

Doctors state that the chance of developing an infection as severe as Edington's is rare. Lesser infections are pretty common, however, and this is something that anyone who is thinking about getting a piercing should consider.

Rejection and Migration

While piercings can lead to many of the same conditions as tattoos (including allergic reactions and keloids), there are also differences. Sometimes, after a piercing the body does not accept the piece of jewelry or other object that is placed into the hole. The result of this is migration or rejection of the piercing. In both cases scarring is a likely side effect.

Migration is when the piercing moves, on its own, from the original location to a new location. This process can be painful, or it can go unnoticed. During this process the piercing slowly moves from the initial spot, settles in a new area, and heals in that spot. A person ends up with a piercing in a different location than they had planned. According to Elayne Angel, "The piercing is likely to migrate when unsuitable or insufficient tissue is pierced, or if your jewelry is too small in diameter, thin in gauge, or of poor quality. Inexperienced and untrained piercers often make these errors."[22]

Rejection occurs when the body senses a foreign object—in this case the jewelry—and feels it is dangerous, so the body pushes it out. Once the jewelry comes out, the skin grows back over the opening. When this occurs, a person typically develops a scar. Angel writes that rejection results from the same causes as migration.

Surface piercings, piercings that are deliberately shallow, are much more prone to migration and rejection than are typical piercings. This is because there is less skin available to keep the piercing in place. In all cases Angel recommends removing the piercing if signs of migration or rejection are occurring. This will reduce the chances of scarring and allow healing to occur.

Blowouts

A unique type of piercing called stretching can result in a complication termed a "blowout." Stretching is when individuals continue to increase their earring size until they have developed a large fistula, or tunnel, through the earlobe. If done properly, stretching typically takes several months. When the earlobe is stretched too quickly, blowouts can occur. A blowout is when part of the earlobe is forced out of the tunnel over the outside of the piercing. The result is that a small flap of skin folds over the outer edge of the piercing. If not taken care of, the small flap can increase in size.

Piercing professionals recommend that, in the case of a blowout, the person reduce the size of his or her jewelry to allow the blowout to be reabsorbed into the body. If this does not occur, a blowout may need to be repaired by a surgeon.

Darkening of the Skin

A few weeks after getting her navel pierced, Amber (last name not given) wrote to Elayne Angel to ask for advice. Amber had discovered that a dark-colored circle had formed around her navel. Angel replied that this is not abnormal, but also is not entirely reversible. Hyperpigmentation, the darkening of skin, is how some bodies naturally respond to the trauma of a piercing. There are some chemicals that can be used to decrease the shade, but these cannot make it fade entirely.

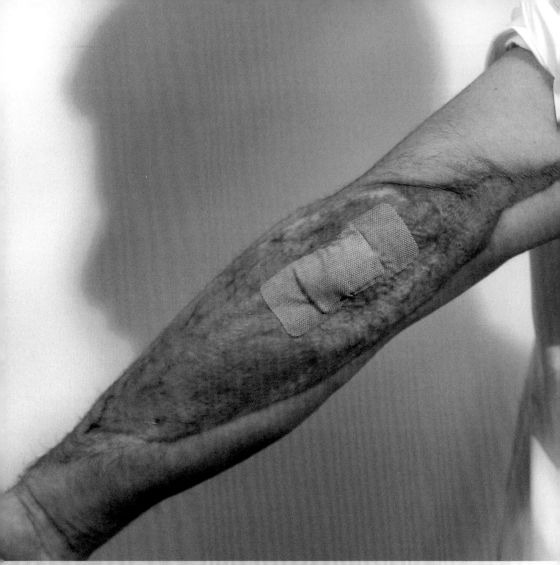

Necrotizing fasciitis, also known as flesh-eating bacteria, destroys skin tissue as can be seen in this photograph. One young woman in Indiana developed this condition in one of her breasts after getting her nipples pierced.

Choosing Jewelry Carefully

There are a variety of ways people can reduce their chances of developing a piercing-related problem. Choosing proper jewelry is one way to prevent problems. According to the Association of Professional Piercers, "The look of the jewelry that is placed in your fresh piercing must be secondary to aspects that affect safety and compatibility with your body. The size, style, material, and quality of the initial piece of jewelry all affect your ability to heal."[23]

One size does not fit all with jewelry. Size should be determined by the location of the piercing and individual physical characteristics. For example, 14 gauge (thickness) jewelry is recommended for a navel piercing, whereas 18 gauge jewelry is recommended for a nostril piercing. The smaller the gauge number, the thicker the jewelry. A nostril requires a smaller hole than a navel piercing. The length of the jewelry must also be considered. A person who is getting a tongue piercing and has a thick tongue will require a longer barbell piece than someone whose tongue is not as thick. If the wrong size jewelry is chosen, a person is at higher risk of rejection, migration, and infection. As an example, when jewelry is too thin for a person's body part, the body treats it as a foreign object, like a splinter, and tries to get rid of it.

Choosing the wrong type of jewelry will also negatively affect a piercing. For example, a tongue piercing requires a barbell type of jewelry, whereas a nostril screw should be used when getting a nostril piercing. As with the wrong size, rejection, migration, and infection can occur if the wrong type of jewelry is inserted. Professionals recommend that a person getting pierced allow a licensed body artist to help choose the jewelry type and size because of their experience and knowledge.

The type of material used in the jewelry can also be important because certain materials are less likely to produce an allergic reaction. Titanium, gold, and stainless steel are among the recommended materials, especially while a piercing is healing.

Avoid Piercing Guns

Another way to prevent piercing problems is to avoid piercing guns. A piercing gun is a mechanical device that is designed to pierce earlobes by forcing a stud earring through the lobe as the piercer squeezes the gun. For years, girls who wanted to get their earlobes pierced have typically visited mall or jewelry stores, where an employee used a piercing gun to make the holes. Some stores also use piercing guns for ear cartilage and nostril

<aside>
Did You Know?

In the state of Oklahoma, to become a licensed body piercer a person must provide proof that he or she is CPR certified, has completed a blood-borne pathogens course, has completed first-aid certification, and has completed an apprentice course or two years working as a licensed practitioner in another state.
</aside>

piercing, although these devices are intended only for use in piercing earlobes.

The Association of Professional Piercers recommends that people do not get any type of piercing with a piercing gun. One reason is that not every part of a piercing gun can be taken apart and sterilized in between piercings. This increases the chances of transmitting viruses and bacteria from one person to another. Another reason to avoid piercing guns is that they only use a standard jewelry size. People with thicker earlobes might find their earrings are too tight, which could lead to swelling. In contrast, a professional piercer has access to different sizes of jewelry and the knowledge to choose the right size for each client.

One last reason to avoid piercing guns is that they typically force regular, blunt-ended studs through the earlobes. This can cause pain or trauma, whereas a piercing professional will use a razor-sharp, hollow needle that slices through the skin quickly and decreases the likelihood of damaging the tissue around it.

How Laws Try to Prevent Health Problems

Many states have adopted laws to protect both the piercing professional and the consumer. These laws typically deal with health-related issues. For example, many states require that body piercing studios register with local health departments. By doing so, they are expected to comply with health department regulations on proper disposal of medical waste and on sterilization procedures, as well as submit to regular inspections.

Some states have additional rules for body piercing practitioners. In North Carolina and other states, for instance, they are required to wear disposable rubber gloves during all procedures. They must use an autoclave to sterilize equipment and also ensure they sterilize a client's skin before starting any procedure. Operators also must prove they are

CPR qualified and have an up-to-date certificate stating they have been trained in blood-borne pathogens.

For these reasons, the best way to prevent health problems from piercing is to have work done only at a licensed studio. Although there are still health risks, by going to a licensed studio these risks are significantly mitigated. Anyone considering body piercing should, according to the Association of Body Piercers, carefully choose who they are getting pierced by and understand what effects can occur from piercing before making a decision.

Chapter Four

Body Art for Health and Well-Being

Tattoos and piercings are most often a form of personal adornment or an expression of individuality. But medical professionals—and their patients—are turning to tattoos and piercings for a variety of physical and mental health needs.

A Tongue Piercing Makes Movement Possible

For many people who have suffered severe spinal cord injuries, the tongue is one of the few body parts they are able to control. Researchers have combined the tongue's ability to move with tongue piercings in an effort to give quadriplegics more mobility. Georgia Institute of Technology engineers have developed the Tongue Drive System (TDS), which is a wireless, wearable device that allows users to operate computers and electric wheelchairs with their tongues.

Previously, older versions of TDS were worn externally, as a headset. However, any shift of the headset resulted in the whole system needing recalibration. By moving the system into the mouth, this problem is avoided, which gives the user more control. A dental appliance is worn in the mouth and is molded to fit tightly around the person's teeth. This device senses movement from a magnet that is placed on a tongue piercing. The user moves his or her tongue in a specific direction. The device then uses this movement to transmit data that can control a computer cursor or work as a joystick to control an electric wheelchair.

In early trials the magnet was glued to the participant's mouth, but the adhesive did not last long; magnets fell off within hours. That is when researchers came up with the idea of piercing the tongue and inserting a stud topped with a magnet. Clinical trials are ongoing for the device. Ann Carias, a student involved in the research who is tattooed and pierced for cosmetic reasons, believes the technology will give disabled people more freedom. "I think it's great that something taboo can be used for therapeutic reasons,"[24] she says.

A Tattoo for Diabetics

Tattoos are also finding useful medical purposes. For example, many people with diabetes would be relieved if they could reduce the number of times they must prick their bodies to test their blood sugar levels. Tattoos may help them with this problem.

Diabetes is a condition in which the body does not properly process food for use as energy. Most food that people eat is turned into glucose, or sugar, for energy. The body relies on the hormone insulin, which is made by the pancreas, to help glucose pass into the cells. When someone has diabetes, his or her body either does not make enough insulin or cannot use its own insulin the way it should. This results in a buildup of sugars in the blood. Depending on the severity of their disease, people with diabetes may regulate their glucose through medications, insulin shots, and/or diet. No matter how they regulate their disease, all diabetics need to monitor their glucose levels by pricking their skin and checking their blood. This helps them determine what to do to keep their glucose in check.

A new type of tattoo, called a nano-ink tattoo, may be able to help diabetics reduce the number of times they need to prick themselves to test their blood. This idea is still in development, but essentially it involves "nano particles with a dye inside of them, and they're inserted into a skin as would be a tattoo,"[25] explains Texas Diabetes Institute research associate Curtiss

A tiny magnet placed in a pierced tongue (pictured) may help some quadriplegics to achieve mobility. The magnet turns the tongue into a joystick that can operate a computer or a wheelchair.

Puckett. Once inserted into the skin, the tattoo detects glucose levels and turns yellow or orange, depending on what the level is. The tattoo can only be seen by positioning a device over it that reveals its color. The darker the color, the lower the person's glucose. Researchers believe this device will eventually give diabetics another way to monitor their blood glucose levels.

Covering Scars

A different use for tattoos is to help people cosmetically cover up physical flaws such as scars from injuries or surgeries. These scars can cause emotional pain because of how they look and/or because they may be a painful reminder of a traumatic event. Tattoos can help people cover up scars and even turn their scars into something aesthetically pleasing to them.

Singer and actress Demi Lovato endured depression and intense emotional swings as a youth. This led her to begin cutting herself starting at age eleven and throughout her teens. Though she recovered from both the physical and emotional trauma of this time, her scars remain. She eventually opted to tattoo over her wrist scars as a way to remind herself that she survived. She has said that the words she tattooed over the scars give her something more positive to look at, rather than marks from the self-harming. "My tattoos say 'Stay strong.' 'Stay' on one [wrist] and 'strong' on the other. Now I'm able to look at them and be thankful for being alive,"[26] she states.

Other people incorporate their scars into their tattoos to turn a reminder of crisis into a display of power. Jane (last name not given) decided to get a tattoo that highlights her scar from a mastectomy that she underwent as she battled breast cancer. At Dragonfly Ink Studio in San

Floral Head

Ann McDonald has alopecia. About three years before her sixtieth birthday, she lost all of her hair. For years she was so depressed that there were days she did not want to get out of bed. She tried wigs and hats, but none of them made her feel better. She happened to be searching the Internet one day when she found a woman who had tattooed her entire head. McDonald decided that was what she would do too. The journey to a head tattoo was not easy. Several tattoo studios turned her down because they thought the process was too dangerous. McDonald persevered and found a studio that agreed to do the piece. The process was painful and long, but McDonald endured because she knew it was what she wanted. After four three-hour sessions, her head was covered with floral and spiral shadings over a black background. "People at work think it's fantastic and take pictures of it. Ian [McDonald's husband] likes it and my family like it. I feel so much happier—it feels so much better than wearing a wig," McDonald says.

Quoted in Katy Winter, "Grandmother-of-Three Faces Up to Her Hair Loss in an Unusual Way . . . by Getting Her Entire HEAD Covered in a £700 Tattoo," *Daily Mail* (London), December 3, 2012. www.dailymail.co.uk.

Francisco, California, she got tattooed with a lizard that uses her scar for its spine. "The entire process was wonderful, lizards have always had a special meaning for me and I wanted to use that symbol, with all its rich, very personal and empowering energy,"[27] Jane says. The tattoo has helped her celebrate her life and turned her scar into something that gives her a sense of power.

Restoring Appearances

While some people choose to incorporate their scars into a tattoo, others only want to restore the appearance of unscarred skin. In some cases this can be done with tattoos. Frank Harmon, of Tampa, Florida, underwent chemotherapy, radiation, and surgery after being diagnosed with breast cancer. (Although breast cancer is most common in women, it does occur in a small percentage of men as well.) The result of Harmon's treatments was heavy scarring. "I have a scar across my chest, armpit to armpit, and resigned myself that I'm going to look pretty weird for the rest of my life,"[28] he says. At first Harmon did not want to cover his scar with a tattoo because he had never wanted a tattoo, but then he discovered he could get a tattoo that blended in with his skin.

Tattoo artist Melany Whitney explained that scars can be covered using "invisible ink." "It's basically tattooing, but I'm using permanent cosmetic pigment and not tattoo ink. I mix and blend camouflaged colors to match the skin around the area that is not hypo pigmented, under pigmented or lost its color,"[29] she says. By doing this she is able to cover many scars so that they blend in with the person's skin tone.

Tammy Wedel, a cosmetic tattoo artist, worked on Harmon for just an hour as she created a more natural look on his chest. Harmon was pleased with the results because it restored part of his original skin tone. "As far as what Tammy had done, I see it as kind of putting back what's been taken away. I'm glad to have it done,"[30] he says of the results.

Cosmetic Tattoos

Tattoos can also be used to create or supplement the look of certain parts of the body, such as lip color or hair that people have lost to diseases or other health issues. This is accomplished by micropigmentation, also known as cosmetic tattooing. Cosmetic tattooing involves the same procedure as decorative tattoos, but instead of inking a picture or words on the person's skin, the process is used to ink permanent makeup such as eyebrow shading, lip liner, and eyeliner.

Singer and actress Demi Lovato experienced depression and intense mood swings in her youth and began cutting herself. Now she has tattoos over the scars (visible on her wrists and forearms) to remind herself that she survived this painful period.

Changing Lives

Vinnie Myers, age fifty, from Baltimore, Maryland, has spent more than a decade learning the art of tattooing three-dimensional nipples and areolas to help give breast cancer patients back part of what they lost to mastectomies. In 2001, while Myers was working as a tattoo artist in a typical studio, a local plastic surgeon contacted him and asked him to help women who had undergone reconstructive breast surgery. Since then Myers has dedicated himself to improving the process and creating realistic nipples and areolas for women. Myers estimates that he has completed around two thousand to three thousand breast tattoos in the past ten years and has attracted clients from as far away as Saudi Arabia and Brazil. According to Myers, "I do look forward to each new day and the chance to change the way my clients look and feel."

Vinnie Myers, "Been a Time Since I Last Posted," *Tattoos by Vinnie Myers* (blog), September 7, 2012. http://vinniemyers.webs.com.

As with standard tattooing, cosmetic tattooing is not regulated by the federal government. However, most states require cosmetic tattooists or studios to obtain licenses. These licenses require that the practitioners follow local health codes, and some require specific professional training. The Society of Permanent Cosmetic Professionals guides those interested in working with permanent makeup by providing articles about the profession and access to training programs. Many who become cosmetic tattooists obtain professional certification in micropigmentation through classes provided by different organizations.

Skin Camouflage

Cosmetic tattoos can be used to help people who have suffered from medical problems that have affected how they look. One of these problems is vitiligo, a skin condition where people lose some of their original skin color pigment. The destruction of these pigments is thought to be related to an immune problem, but at this time researchers have not found a definite cause. About 1 percent of the world's population is afflicted with vitiligo, and the average person afflicted first develops it in his or her mid-twenties.

Vitiligo can damage people's self-esteem because it often significantly changes how they look. Cosmetic tattooing provides a way to camouflage the affected areas on certain parts of a person's body. During the process a special surgical instrument is used to implant pigments into a patient's skin to give color to the areas where they have lost natural skin pigments. According to the Mayo Clinic, micropigmentation is most effective around the lips and in people with darker skin. The procedure does not stop the spread of vitiligo, but it camouflages the skin that has already been affected.

A study on the effectiveness of tattooing as a treatment of lip vitiligo by the Department of Plastic & Reconstructive Surgery at Chhatrapati Shahuji Maharaj Medical University in India was completed in 2008. The study included fifteen lip vitiligo patients whose ages ranged from thirty to fifty-five years. They all underwent the micropigmentation process under local anesthesia. Each patient was seen again after two to three years to assess the results, and in all cases their cosmetic appearance remained improved compared to how they looked before the treatment.

Tattooing Hair

Hair loss is a natural occurrence as men, and sometimes women, age. But in some people hair loss is more than a natural progression. Alopecia areata is a common autoimmune skin disease that results in the loss of hair on the scalp and elsewhere on the body. It usually starts with one or more small, round, smooth patches on the scalp and can progress to total scalp hair loss (alopecia totalis) or complete body hair loss (alopecia universalis). Tattoos can be helpful to some of those who have this condition.

Some people with alopecia have turned to cosmetic tattooing as a way to restore the look of lost eyebrows. The tattooing of hair is performed in the same way as a regular tattoo. The cosmetic tattooist uses a needle to deposit pigments into the dermal layer of the skin. He or she chooses pigments that replicate the shade of

Did You Know?
About 5 million people in the United States live with vitiligo, according to the National Vitiligo Foundation.

a person's natural hair color and then places the pigments into the shape of eyebrows.

Scott MacMillan of the United Kingdom is one of the many alopecia sufferers who has benefited from cosmetic tattooing. At just sixteen, his hair started to fall out in clumps. He grew his hair long on the sides to hide the bald patches, but by the time he was twenty-two he had lost all of his hair, and by age twenty-six he had also lost his eyebrows and eyelashes. By age forty-five he had come to terms with his hair loss, but still had difficulty accepting the loss of his eyebrows and eyelashes. That is when he decided to investigate cosmetic tattooing. "I came to terms with my baldness years ago—but losing my eyebrows was difficult. The tattoos have transformed the way I look. I wish I'd done it years ago,"[31] MacMillan said.

A New Head of Hair

Tattooing can also be used to help men undergoing normal hair loss. The procedure is not simple, however. It can take many hours. In 2012 several companies offered a new procedure to give bald people "hair" via a tattoo method. The method, known as MHT (micro hair technique) scalp pigmentation or SMP (scalp micropigmentation), involves tattooing different shades of pigments on the scalp so that they represent the size, shape, and density of short hairs. The result is the look of a buzz cut. The process typically takes two to three sessions, each four to six hours long, spaced about a week apart. The main differences between this process and the process involved in getting a normal tattoo is that the needles do not penetrate as deeply as typical tattoo needles, and instead of tattoo inks, specialized pigments that do not bleed or change colors are used.

Celebrity hairdresser Adee Phelan started losing his hair in his twenties due to male pattern baldness. He decided to undergo MHT and is pleased with the results. "I thought losing my hair didn't bother me but even I felt younger and more confident after [the MHT process]. And it looks so natural, most people don't even know I've had it done,"[32] says Phelan.

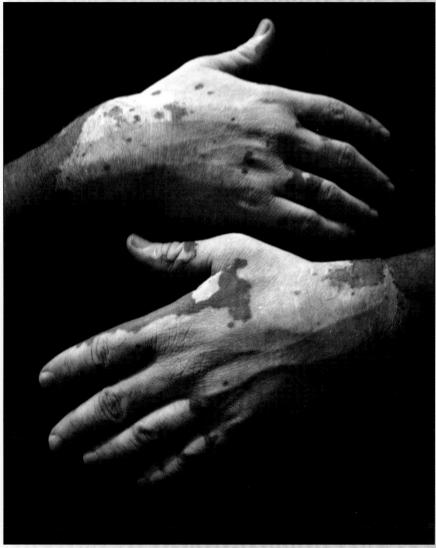

Tattoo practitioners have been able to help people with vitiligo, a skin condition that causes loss of pigment and results in irregular patches of pale skin. Cosmetic tattooing can help to camouflage the affected areas.

Breast Reconstruction

Cosmetic tattooing also helps women who have undergone mastectomies. A mastectomy is the surgical removal of a woman's breast, usually as part of treatment for breast cancer. Many women who undergo mastectomies also undergo breast reconstruction. While doctors today can create a remarkably natural-looking breast, they cannot replicate the areola, which is the dark skin that surrounds the nipples. A trained cosmetic tattoo artist can create a natural-looking areola on each breast, however. First, the cosmetic tattooist carefully chooses colors that he or she will tattoo onto the breast in order to create the areola. If the patient is matching a new areola to one on an existing breast, the tattooist will mix various colors and shades to get the correct pigment. If both breasts were reconstructed, the tattooist will use preoperative photos of the patient's natural breasts to recreate the nipple color or choose a new color that matches the patient's skin tones. When tattooing, the artist also creates the illusion of a nipple by making the central area of the areola darker than the outer circle. This process can be done only after the reconstruction has fully healed.

Sasha Merritt, owner and artist of the Dragonfly Ink Studio in San Francisco, works closely with many breast cancer survivors and finds that they respond to their tattoos with a newfound confidence. According to one client, Wendy (last name not given), "Now when I see myself, my first thought isn't to feel sorry I had breast cancer, but 'Gee! I have good looking breasts."[33] Because she has seen how women respond to her work, Merritt honors National Breast Cancer Awareness Month each October by offering a free areola repigmentation clinic for women who cannot otherwise afford the procedure.

Reclaiming Their Bodies

Physical problems are not the only ones that can be addressed with body art. People have found that certain types of body art can help with emotional healing, too. Specifically, some women who have suffered physical trauma have discovered that body piercing can aid emotional healing.

Elayne Angel says that she has received many e-mails from women who were sexually abused and used piercing as way to take control of their bodies. One young woman wrote to Angel about the experience of getting a genital piercing on her eighteenth birthday. "I was sexually abused for five years when I was a kid so my body never did feel like it was completely mine until my birthday," the young woman wrote. "I feel so liberated, new, fresh and like I finally have a choice with my body—I never knew a piercing could make someone feel this way or could help me out much more than any therapist could."[34] Others have written Angel with similar stories about how piercings have helped give them a sense of power and the ability to overcome what they have suffered.

People around the world are benefiting from the latest findings of what permanent body art can do to improve health and well-being. The opportunities for tattoos and body piercings to help people are increasing with the discovery of new uses for them. Many are excited about the potential of body art to improve people's emotional and physical lives.

Chapter Five

Removal Challenges

Not everyone who gets body art remains happy with his or her decision. Changes in their lives or bodies may result in people regretting their tattoos and piercings. Some types of body art can be easily removed. Other types require procedures that carry risks or that might not be entirely successful.

Who Is Dissatisfied and Why?

Although most people are initially pleased with their tattoos, surveys have found that between 10 and 35 percent of tattooed individuals eventually wish they could reverse their decision to get inked. A 2012 Harris Poll found that 14 percent of tattooed individuals in the United States regret their decision to get tattoos. In the United Kingdom a 2012 survey by East Lancashire Hospitals NHS Trust regarding people's feelings about their tattoos found that nearly one-third of those surveyed regretted their tattoos. The same survey found that tattoo regret was three times more likely among men if they got their tattoo before age sixteen.

Body piercing also results in regrets. One Mayo Clinic study found that nearly half of college students with tongue piercings eventually let them close. Texas Tech University School of Health and Sciences Center conducted another study of body piercing trends among college students in 2007. This study found that 13 to 18 percent of piercings obtained in years prior to the survey had been permanently removed by the time of the survey. The percentage was higher among upperclassmen.

Another type of body art related to piercings can also result in great regret. Many plastic surgeons are seeing an increase in earlobe repair requests from people who have gauged their earlobes. Gauging, the stretching of body parts with piercing jewelry, cannot be covered or taken out like a typical piercing. People with gauged earlobes have encountered negative reactions by others, particularly in the workplace.

There are many other reasons people come to regret their piercings and tattoos. For some, the tattoo or piercing no longer symbolizes something important in their lives, or they just do not like the way it looks anymore. Others experience repeated problems with allergic reactions and infections related to their body art. But one of the main reasons cited for regret is the impact that body art has on careers. "Today, many college-aged people are getting visible tattoos like anchors, owls and obnoxiously big blue butterflies. However, in the real world, most employers think negatively about hiring people with visible tattoos,"[35] writes Paige Jurgensen, who sports four tattoos, all of which are easily covered with clothing. Jurgensen, however, decided against getting a tattoo on her wrist because it would be more difficult to conceal once she starts looking for a job after college.

Laser Tattoo Removal

The most common, and most successful, method for removing tattoos involves the use of a laser. A dermatologist usually does this procedure. The laser produces short pulses of light that penetrate the top layers of the tattooed skin, searching for contrast between skin tone and ink. When the lasers find this contrast, they pulse intensely on the ink pigments but not the skin's natural pigments. As the tattoo pigments absorb the pulses of light, they break into smaller particles. Over time the immune system removes the particles by breaking them down even further and flushing them out of the body. Typically, it takes multiple sessions to remove a tattoo. The number of sessions usually depends on the type of ink that was used and how deeply the tattoo artist injected it. Most health professionals recommend three weeks between sessions to allow the pigment particles to be absorbed.

The success of tattoo removal depends on several factors. A 2012 Italian study published in the *Archives of Dermatology* discussed why certain

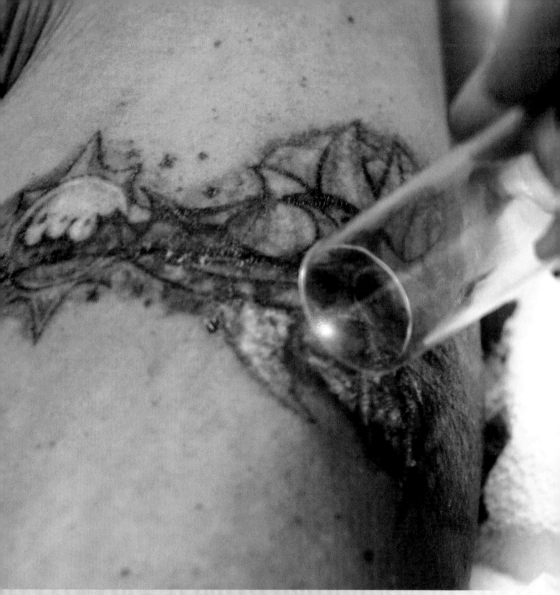

A plastic surgeon uses a laser to remove the black ink from a tattoo. People who got tattoos when they were young sometimes later regret their actions and undergo removal procedures that can be painful and expensive.

tattoos could be removed more easily than others. The Italian researchers documented the results of laser removal treatment of 352 people between 1995 and 2010 and explored factors that make some tattoos harder to remove than others. During the study, researchers found that the lasers removed tattoos for 47 percent of all the patients in ten sessions, and an additional 28 percent of patients' tattoos were successfully removed with five more sessions.

The color of the tattoo has a major effect on removal success. Because black pigment absorbs all laser wavelengths, it is the easiest to remove. In the study, 58 percent of tattoos that were done in black were removed in ten sessions. Fifty-one percent of red and black tattoos were also removed in ten sessions. Other colors, such as green, are more difficult to remove because they cannot absorb all laser wavelengths. Colors such as purple and yellow can be the most difficult to remove because there is less contrast between the skin tone and ink, which makes it difficult for the lasers to identify the ink. Dr. Paul Jarrod Frank, the founder and director of 5th Avenue Dermatology Surgery and Laser Center, says, "Patients with tattoos with those colors, I actually try to convince them not to remove it."[36]

The study also found that smokers with tattoos are less likely to obtain success with laser tattoo removal. This is due to the fact that smoking interferes with the immune system and impedes the healing of wounds, which affects the success of tattoo removal. In the study, smokers had a 70 percent lower chance than nonsmokers of successful tattoo removal in ten treatments. Most needed additional treatments to remove their tattoos.

A tattoo's age also affects whether it can be successfully removed or not. During the study, tattoos older than thirty-six months were more difficult to remove. This is due to the fact that ink particles migrate into deeper layers of the skin over time. Removing these tattoos in most cases is possible but may take more sessions.

Tattoo Drawbacks

In addition to taking into consideration whether or not laser tattoo removal will be effective, people with tattoos need to consider other issues before undergoing the removal process. One is cost. An average session can cost $200, and most dermatologists state that three or more sessions are required to remove most tattoos.

Another drawback is pain; the procedure is not painless. Some people say the removal pain is worse

Did You Know?
According to the Patient's Guide, a family of twenty-five medical web publications, the majority of people having tattoos removed cited employment reasons as their motivation for having the procedure.

than the tattoo application pain. Often a person undergoing the procedure feels a sustained hot, stinging sensation. Tricia R. was willing to endure the pain and cost to rid herself of a large tattoo she got on her lower back when she was nineteen. She referred to the tattoo as a "tramp stamp," a pejorative term for tattoos that women get on their lower back. She came to regret her tattoo shortly after getting it, when she joined organizations and activities at college and became embarrassed by the unprofessional look of the tattoo. Despite the fact that doctors estimated it would take twenty sessions, thousands of dollars, and significant pain to rid herself of the tattoo, she opted to undergo removal. "I immediately felt like I was being pelted with hot grease and flicked with rubber bands," Tricia said after the sixth removal session. "It by far is the worst pain I have ever felt in my entire life. On top of the pain, the noise of the laser burning my skin is similar to the noise of bacon frying in a skillet."[37]

> **Did You Know?**
>
> In a study conducted by the Patient's Guide, the number of tattoo removal procedures grew by 32 percent from 2011 to 2012.

Other Options

Although laser tattoo removal is the most common way to erase tattoos, there are other options. Among these options are surgical incision, dermabrasion, and cryosurgery. These methods have some advantages over laser removal, but they also have side effects that many people find undesirable. During surgical incision, the patient is anesthetized while a doctor uses a scalpel to cut out the tattoo. For small tattoos, the surgeon can stitch the skin closed. However, larger tattoos may require a skin graft to cover the area of skin that was removed. The reason some choose this option is that the tattoo can be entirely removed, leaving no remnants. A major risk with this process is that it typically results in a scar. This process is also quite expensive, ranging from $3,000 to $10,000, depending on the size of the tattoo and whether a skin graft is required.

Tamra Barney, who starred in the reality TV show *The Real Housewives of Orange County*, attempted to remove a tattoo of her ex-husband's name, Simon, from her finger by laser removal but was not happy with the results. "The laser did lighten and blur my tattoo, but chances were it would never [be] removed it completely," Barney says. "The tattoo of Simon's name was a constant reminder of my past and needed to be removed for good."[38] She decided to undergo surgical incision, which completely removed the tattoo.

Another removal option is dermabrasion, which is when a dermatologist scrapes away the surface and middle layers of the tattoo with a high-speed rotary device that has an abrasive wheel or brush. This technique is referred to as "sanding." During the process a patient is often given a sedative to help him or her remain calm, and the skin is anesthetized. For a few days after the process, the skin will feel burned and

Tattoo Nightmares

Getting a tattoo blindfolded is not a good idea, but Marshall (last name not given) did it anyway. While out partying one night, he and his friend Kara saw that a tattoo shop was running a special—get a tattoo blindfolded and the tattoo is free. Intoxicated and encouraged by his friend, who was also intoxicated, he agreed to the deal. Several minutes later, he realized he had made a mistake. Marshall recalls, "I'm sitting there blindfolded and Kara's being real quiet, which is odd, 'cuz normally she's a loud drunk." When they took his blindfold off, Kara revealed that the tattoo studio had her, untrained in tattooing, ink a large tribal tattoo on his forearm. With an ugly reminder of that night on his arm, for years Marshall regretted his decision.

Eventually, he ended up on Spike TV's *Tattoo Nightmares* show, which features professional tattoo artists transforming poorly done tattoos into professional-looking ones. On the show, tattoo artist Jasmine Rodriguez was chosen to work on Marshall's tattoo, and she said this large black tattoo was the most difficult cover-up she had ever done. However, luckily for Marshall, she managed to transform his tribal ink into an image of the Four Horsemen of the Apocalypse.

"'Tattoo Nightmares': Man's Drunk Friend Gave Him a Huge Tribal," *Huffington Post*, October 31, 2012. www.huffingtonpost.com.

irritated, but typically the skin heals within ten days. Several treatment sessions are usually necessary to remove the tattoo. The risks of this process are that scarring may occur and the skin may develop different dark or light patches in the area that was scraped. Dermabrasion cost depends on the size of the tattoo and location on the body, but typically runs from $1,000 to $4,000.

A more affordable and less invasive surgery than excision or dermabrasion is cryosurgery. Cryosurgery typically runs in the hundreds of dollars versus thousands. During this procedure the tattooed area is sprayed with liquid nitrogen that freezes the skin and destroys the tattooed tissues, which are then peeled away. The main problems associated with cryosurgery are that it can leave flat white spots in the area, it may damage nearby healthy tissue, and it may even harm nerve tissue.

Closing Body Piercings

Removal of body piercings is generally a more straightforward and less costly process than removing tattoos. The process typically does not require outside help and does not cost anything. However, the body part may not be completely restored to its former state after the piercing is removed.

According to professional body artists, to remove most piercings, the person should first ensure that the piercing is completely healthy, without infections. Allowing an infected piercing to close will trap the infection in the body. Once it is determined that the piercing is healthy, the person can just remove the earring, stud, or other object that was inserted in the hole. The location of the hole should be washed gently once a day and antibiotic cream applied multiple times a day. During this time frame the piercing may secrete sebum, a white liquid; as long as it is not accompanied by swelling or itching, it is not a problem. The amount of time it takes a piercing to close depends on where the piercing is located. It can take anywhere from a week to several months.

How the body part looks once the hole closes depends on the size of the hole, where it was made,

Many piercings can be closed fairly easily by simply removing the jewelry and letting the holes close on their own. Microdermals, which are single-point piercings, and stretched earlobes (both of which can be seen here) are more complicated to undo.

and how old the piercing is. Tongue piercings close up relatively quickly and with minimal problems, whereas an eyebrow piercing can take months to close. Older piercings take longer to close than newer piercings. Even after the hole fully closes, the area where it healed might look different than it did before the piercing. Some scarring and lumpy,

Industry Growth

Regrets about tattoos and piercings and efforts to have them re-moved have benefited at least two groups: plastic surgeons and tattoo removal businesses. Dr. Glenn Messina, a tattoo removal specialist and owner of Messina Esthetic Medicine in New York, has seen a significant increase in his business over the last few years. Messina says his tattoo removal business has increased by 15 percent due to the increased number of people who want to rid themselves of tattoos. Plastic surgeons have also seen an increase in work due to body art. Dr. David Kahn, a plastic sur-geon in California, first repaired stretched ears in 2010 and has seen a significant increase in the number of clients coming in for this type of surgery.

discolored keloids are not uncommon, especially with earlobe piercings. Also, piercers recommend that people think carefully before closing their piercings, because if they ever want to repierce in the same area, scar tissue from the old piercing may make it difficult.

Microdermals

Although most piercings can be closed without going to a professional, more complicated piercings, such as microdermals, should not be re-moved by the person wearing them. This is because microdermals are single-point piercings where instead of going in one end of the skin and coming out the other, they go in one end and then are anchored under-neath the skin. To take out the jewelry, a person's skin must be cut open with a scalpel, and forceps are usually used to extract the jewelry. Only a licensed practitioner or a doctor should do this procedure.

In 2009 Amber Hutcheson, who has several piercings and tattoos, decided to have both of her cheek microdermals surgically removed because they were causing her pain. Hutcheson posted a video of the removal process online. She went to a piercing studio to have the mi-crodermals removed, and during the process the body art practitioner wore gloves and used sterilized instruments. Each removal took just a few minutes with a minimal amount of bleeding. After the removal of the first cheek microdermal was completed, Hutcheson commented, "No more microdermals for me."[39]

Stretching Closure

Whereas typical body piercings have a good chance of closing, earlobes that have been stretched are more difficult to fix. The tunnels in the skin that are developed by stretching, also known as gauging, may not close on their own after the jewelry is taken out. Instead, surgery may be required.

Small gauged (or stretched) earlobes can be slowly undone by inserting smaller and smaller jewelry in the hole. But some gauging can only be undone through plastic surgery.

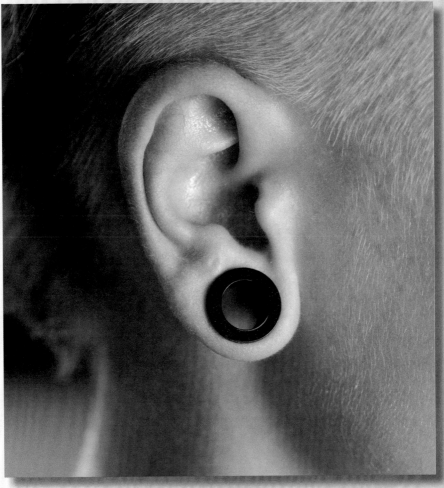

Body art professionals say that it is possible for stretching to go back to normal without surgery, but this depends on several factors. "If you stretched slowly and carefully, not causing any tearing or scarring, that will increase your chances of your ear going back to its normal size and shape. If you used a dermal punch, stretched too quickly, used heavy weights that stretched an abnormal shape or caused any scar tissue to form, then your likelihood of it going back is greatly diminished,"[40] writes Karen Hudson, author of *Living Canvas: Your Complete Guide to Tattoos, Piercings, and Body Modification*. Also a factor is how long the stretched body part has been healed since the original stretching. The longer it has been healed the less likely it is that it will return to its normal shape.

Closing a gauged earlobe without surgery can take time. Body piercers say the best way to do this is to gradually decrease the size of the piercing jewelry. Over time, sometimes weeks, the skin will shrink to the new, smaller jewelry size. Once this happens, the person can then repeat the process using a smaller and smaller piece of jewelry each time. Eventually, the jewelry can be removed and the hole allowed to close.

Landon Rochat-Boeser realized at age twenty-four that it was time to close his stretched earlobes after ten years of increasing the disc size of his jewelry. "It's not that I regret it, but this is a different time in my life," Rochat-Boeser said. "If I want to be taken seriously as a professional, I have to start looking like a professional. Whether you like it or not, or whether it's fair or not, people judge you based on your appearance."[41] Rochat-Boeser ended up paying for surgery because his earlobes were stretched too far to contract on their own.

The surgery is not complicated, according to Maryland plastic surgeon Jeffrey E. Schreiber. The process involves the patient undergoing local anesthesia while the doctor sutures the earlobe closed. After five to seven days, the sutures are removed. Schreiber states that scarring is minimal. The cost, however, is not. Repairing one earlobe in this way can cost several hundred dollars.

> ## Did You Know?
>
> Piercings done with a dermal punch, a device that works like a hole punch, are less likely to close on their own than an earlobe that has been slowly stretched over time.

Serious Decisions

Despite the cost and potential consequences, many people choose to remove their body art because of their dissatisfaction with its look, a change in their life situation, or how it affects their professional lives. In most cases removal is possible, but it may come with consequences.

Introduction: Pain and Relief

1. Quoted in *Daily Mail* (London), "Woman Who Had Tongue Pierced as Birthday Treat 'Dies of Blood Poisoning Two Days Later,'" April 16, 2012. www.dailymail.co.uk.

2. Quoted in *Daily Mail* (London), "Birthday Tongue Piercing Kills Woman, 34, Within Two Days After She Develops Blood Poisoning," October 14, 2012. www.dailymail.co.uk.

3. Quoted in Evelyn Theiss, "Cosmetic Tattoos Help Clients Deal with Medical Maladies," Cleveland.com, December 31, 2012. www.cleveland.com.

Chapter One: Tattooing and Body Piercing Today

4. Quoted in Megan Neighbor, "Tattoos' Popularity Spurs New Parlors, New Debates," *Arizona Republic* (Phoenix, AZ), July 14, 2010. www.azcentral.com.

5. Quoted in Nora Swearingen, "Piercings Grow in Popularity," *Echo* (Webster Groves, MO), February 2011. http://wgecho.org.

6. Quoted in Swearingen, "Piercings Grow in Popularity."

7. Quoted in Kera Mashek, "Tattoo Artists, Health Officials Concerned About Rise of In-Home Tattooing," Quincy, January 2, 2013. www.wgem.com.

8. Mayo Clinic, "Piercings-How to Prevent Complications," March 6, 2012. www.mayoclinic.com.

9. Quoted in Lloyd de Vries, "Time Off for Pamela Anderson," CBS News, February 11, 2009. www.cbsnews.com.

10. Mayo Clinic, "Nickel Allergy," October 2, 2010. www.mayoclinic.com.

11. Quoted in "CAMBS: Tattoo Was Real Life Saver for Asthma Sufferer," *Hunts Post* (Huntingdon, UK), January 7, 2012. www.huntspost.co.uk.

Chapter Two: Tattoo Health Risks

12. Dragos Roua, "5 Lessons Learned from Getting My First Tattoo," March 16, 2011. www.dragosroua.com.

13. Centers for Disease Control and Prevention, "Basic Information About HIV and AIDS," April 11, 2012. www.cdc.gov.

14. Quoted in Neighbor, "Tattoos' Popularity Spurs New Parlors, New Debates."

15. Quoted in Leon Watson, "Holidaymaker Who Paid £25 for Tattoo in Turkey Faced Having Foot Amputated After It Became Infected," *Daily Mail* (London), August 21, 2012. www.dailymail.co.uk.

16. Quoted in FDA, "Think Before You Ink?," January 30, 2013. www.fda.gov.

17. Quoted in Gene Emery, "Tattoo Infections in U.S. Linked to Contaminated Ink," Reuters, August 22, 2012. www.reuters.com.

18. Gwen Wark, "Tattoo Parlor Requirements," eHow, 2013. www.ehow.com.

Chapter Three: Body Piercing Health Risks

19. Quoted in John Gilt, "Tongue Piercing Gone Terribly Wrong; 15-Year-Old Ends Up in Hospital," Mizozo, May 3, 2012. www.mizozo.com.

20. Shanay, "Horrible Ending to a Birthday Gift . . . ," Belly Button Rings Guide, February 18, 2009. www.belly-button-rings-guide.com.

21. Quoted in "Teen Loses Breast in Piercing Nightmare," *Age* (Melbourne, Australia), October 31, 2006. www.theage.com.au.

22. Elayne Angel, "Questions About Piercing Migration and Rejection," *The Piercing Bible* (blog), April 2011. http://piercingbible.com.

23. Association of Professional Piercers, "Jewelry for Initial Piercings," January 2010. http://safepiercing.org.

Chapter Four: Body Art for Health and Well-Being

24. Quoted in *The Therapeutic Resources* (blog), "Piercing a Tongue in the Name of Mobility," June 9, 2011. http://thetherapeuticresources blog.blogspot.com.

25. Quoted in Jacqueline Ortiz, "'Diabetes Tattoos' May Soon Help Monitor Glucose Levels," WOAI, February 28, 2012. www.woai.com.

26. Quoted in Mark Larkin, "'My Scars Are Battle Wounds': Defiant Demi Lovato on How She Conquered Self-Harming Hell," *Daily Mail* (London), December 3, 2011. www.dailymail.co.uk.

27. Quoted in "Scar Covering with Tattoos," Dragonfly Ink Studio, 2011. http://dragonflyink.com.

28. Quoted in Joette Giovinco, "Tattoo Artists Use Skin-Colored Ink to Hide Scars," MyFox Tampa Bay, November 7, 2012. www.myfox tampabay.com.

29. Quoted in Giovinco, "Tattoo Artists Use Skin-Colored Ink to Hide Scars."

30. Quoted in Giovinco, "Tattoo Artists Use Skin-Colored Ink to Hide Scars."

31. Quoted in Maria Croce, "My Band Is Raising Eyebrows Once Again," *Sun* (London), June 22, 2012. www.thesun.co.uk.

32. Quoted in Maysa Rawi, "Would You Pay £2,000 for Tattooed Hair? Celebrity Stylist Launches New Technique to Disguise Men's Baldness (So Long as You Don't Mind Looking Like a Skinhead)," *Daily Mail* (London), February 10, 2012. www.dailymail.co.uk.

33. Quoted in "Areola and 3D Nipple Reconstruction Tattoos," Dragonfly Ink Studio, 2011. http://dragonflyink.com.

34. Quoted in Elayne Angel, "A Clit Hood (VCH) Piercing to Reclaim Her Body," *The Piercing Bible* (blog), September 27, 2011. http://piercing bible.com.

Chapter Five: Removal Challenges

35. Paige Jurgensen, "Tattoos Can Be an Opportunity Setback," *Linfield Review* (McMinnville, OR), October 2, 2012. www.linfield.edu.

36. Quoted in Sarah Klein, "How to Safely Get a Tattoo Removed," Health.com, November 13, 2009. www.health.com.

37. Quoted in Klein, "How to Safely Get a Tattoo Removed."

38. Tamra Barney, "So Blessed," Bravo TV, May 16, 2012. www.bravotv.com.

39. Amber Hutcheson, "Getting Microdermals Removed," YouTube, May 13, 2009. www.youtube.com.

40. Karen Hudson, "Stretched Earlobes with Gauges," About.com, 2013. http://tattoo.about.com.

41. Quoted in Jeff Strickler, "The Case Against Stretched Earlobes," *Star Tribune* (Minneapolis, MN), January 24, 2012. www.startribune.com.

Books

Elayne Angel, *The Piercing Bible Guide to Aftercare and Troubleshooting.* New York: Random House, 2013.

Genia Gaffaney, *The Art of Body Piercing: Everything You Need to Know Before, During, and After Getting Pierced.* Bloomington, IN: iUniverse, 2013.

Karen Hudson, *Living Canvas: Your Total Guide to Tattoos, Piercings, and Body Modification.* Berkeley, CA: Seal, 2009.

Pete Peterson, *Tattoo Removal: The Modern Guide to Tattoo Removal and Fading.* Seattle, WA: Amazon Digital Services, 2012.

Frank Spalding, *Erasing the Ink: Getting Rid of Your Tattoo.* New York: Rosen, 2011.

Internet Sources

Glenn Braunstein, "Drilling Down on Body Piercing Health Issues," *Huffington Post*, May 21, 2012. www.huffingtonpost.com/glenn-d -braunstein-md/body-piercing_b_1525337.html.

Caroline McClatchey, "Ear Stretching: Why Is Lobe 'Gauging' Growing in Popularity?," BBC, November 21, 2011. www.bbc.co.uk/news/maga zine-15771237.

Amy Mobley and Everett Lehman, "Safety and Health for Tattoo-ists and Piercers," *NIOSH Science Blog*, Centers for Diseases Control and Prevention, October 27, 2009. http://blogs.cdc.gov/niosh-science -blog/2009/10/tattoo.

Courtney Robinson, "Tattoo Removal Business Booming," ABC7, February 27, 2013. www.abc-7.com/story/21420390/tattoo-removal-busi ness-booming.

Websites

Alliance of Professional Tattooists (www.safe-tattoos.com). This website provides information about the tattoo business.

American Academy of Micropigmentation (www.micropigmentation.org). This website provides information about cosmetic tattooing, how to get certified, and how to find a certified micropigmentologist.

Association of Professional Piercers (www.safepiercing.com). This website provides information about safe piercing practices and current piercing legislation.

Centers for Disease Control and Prevention (www.cdc.gov). This website provides health information for the United States and has specific articles regarding tattoos, body piercing, and potential complications.

Mayo Clinic (www.mayoclinic.com). This website provides health information and includes various articles about the health risks of tattoos and body piercings.

Index

Note: Boldface page numbers indicate illustrations.

Picture Credits

Cover: © Markus Cuff/Corbis, Thinkstock Images

AP Images: 23, 40, 46, 49, 58

© Jacek Boczarski/Demotix/Corbis: 63

© Paul Brown/Demotix/Corbis: 15

© Rick Friedman/Corbis: 29

© Catherine Karnow/Corbis: 8

© Abed Rahim Khatib/Demotix/Corbis: 53

Dr. P. Marazzi/Science Photo Library: 34

© Paul Rodriguez/Zuma Press/Corbis: 26

Martin M. Rotker/Science Source: 17

Thinkstock Images: 12, 65

Dr. E. Walker/Science Photo Library: 37

Leanne Currie-McGhee lives in Norfolk, Virginia, with her daughters, Hope and Grace, and husband, Keith. She has enjoyed writing educational books for more than ten years.